Śiva
&
Singularity
NAGARAJ

Copyright Page

ISBN: 9789354695360

First Edition: 2026
Printed in India

DEDICATION

To the silent witness within every reader.

To the mathematicians who seek the Truth in the language of numbers, and the mystics who find the Equations of Light in the stillness of the heart.

May we all return to the Singularity of being.

ACKNOWLEDGMENTS

This work is a bridge built upon the shoulders of giants.

I owe an eternal debt to the ancient seers of the Upaniṣads and the Śaivāgamas, whose inner cartography remains the most sophisticated map of consciousness available to humanity.

My gratitude goes to the pioneers of modern physics—Schrödinger, Heisenberg, Wheeler, and Bohr—who dared to follow the math into the realms of the "weird" and the mystical.

Special thanks to the editors and thinkers who helped refine these complex intersections of Sanskrit and Science into a language accessible to the modern seeker.

Finally, to my family and peers, whose support provided the "Śakti" necessary to bring this "Śiva" of an idea into manifest form.

PREFACE

We live in a fractured age. We have split the atom, but we have also split our own sense of reality. On one side stands Science—objective, cold, and mathematical. On the other stands Spirituality—subjective, warm, and intuitive. We are told we must choose: either a universe of dead matter governed by blind equations, or a universe of spirit that defies logic.

Shiva and Singularity is a refusal of that choice.

This book was born from a simple, startling realization: the "Singularity" that physicists describe at the heart of a Black Hole or at the origin of the Big Bang is the same reality that the ancient Śaiva masters described as the state of Paramaśiva. Both are points of infinite density where time, space, and causality dissolve. Both represent the limit of language and the beginning of absolute potential.

As a researcher of both philosophy and science, I have spent years looking for the "Grand Unified Theory" of experience. What I found was that the deeper we go into the "Micro" (Quantum Physics) and the "Macro" (Cosmology), the more we find the "Internal" (Advaita).

This book is designed to be a print-ready companion for your journey from the head to the heart. It is not an academic treatise, nor is it a religious manual. It is a synthesis. It is a guide for the modern "Techno-Mystic"—the person who values the precision of an equation as much as the depth of a meditation.

Welcome to the bridge. The Singularity is waiting.

TABLE OF CONTENTS

Chapter 1

The Primordial Vibration: Śruti, Spanda, and the Big Bang

Imagine the deepest silence you have ever known. Not just the absence of sound, but the absence of thought, of feeling, of *anything*. A perfect, unblemished void. Now, imagine within that absolute nothingness, a single, infinitesimal throb. A vibration so subtle it is almost imperceptible, yet it contains the blueprint for every galaxy, every star, every atom, and every conscious being that will ever exist.

This paradox—creation emerging from an ultimate stillness—lies at the heart of both ancient Indian cosmology and modern astrophysics. Science describes the "Big Bang" as the singular event that birthed our universe. Indian philosophy speaks of *Spanda*—the primordial vibration, the "throb" of consciousness that manifests all reality.

This chapter is your invitation to explore the profound convergence of these two narratives. We will delve into the oldest known philosophical speculation on creation, the *Nāsādīya Sūkta* of the *Ṛg Veda*, and then compare it with the Standard Cosmological Model. Our aim is not to prove one over the other, but to reveal how these seemingly disparate traditions point to a singular, non-dual source: Śiva.

Understanding this matters because it shifts our perception of reality. The universe is not a dead machine, but a living, breathing expression of consciousness—and you are an intrinsic part of that ongoing vibration.

The Nāsādīya Sūkta: Creation Without Assertion

Long before telescopes peered into distant galaxies or physicists conceived of subatomic particles, the ancient seers (Ṛṣis) of India gazed inward. Their profound contemplations on the origin of the cosmos are enshrined in the *Nāsādīya Sūkta* (Ṛg Veda 10.129), often called the "Hymn of Creation."

This hymn is remarkable for its radical agnosticism and philosophical depth. It begins not with a divine command, but with a series of negations, famously stating:

"Nāsadāsīn no sadāsīt tadānīm" (Then there was neither non-existent nor existent.)

This isn't a declaration of absolute nothingness. Instead, it describes a state beyond human categories of "being" and "non-being." It posits an unmanifest, undifferentiated ground state. It is a mathematical "zero" that is not truly empty, but a plenum of potential.

The hymn continues to negate all familiar aspects of reality—no air, no sky, no death, no immortality. What remained was:

"Ānīdavātaṁ svadhayā tadekam" (That One breathed windless by its own power.)

This "That One" (*Tad Ekam*) is the primordial, uncaused cause. It "breathed" without air, implying a self-existent, self-sufficient pulsation. It is a subtle vibration, not a forceful explosion. This is the ultimate "Singularity" in a philosophical sense—a point beyond description, containing everything.

Spanda Śāstra: The First Throb of Consciousness

In Kashmir Śaivism, a non-dual tradition, this concept of "That One breathing" is elaborated through the **Spanda Śāstra**. *Spanda* literally means "throb," "vibration," or "pulse." It is the fundamental, primordial pulsation of consciousness itself.

Imagine an infinite, perfectly still ocean (Śiva, the static aspect). Within that stillness, there arises a subtle, spontaneous tremor (Śakti, the dynamic aspect). This tremor is *Spanda*. It is not a movement *in* Śiva, but the very nature *of* Śiva to manifest.

- **Śiva:** Pure, unconditioned consciousness (Prakāśa). The ultimate ground of being.

- **Śakti:** The dynamic, creative power of consciousness (Vimarśa). The inherent ability of Śiva to know and express itself.

The *Spanda Kārikā* (1.1) succinctly states: *"Yasyonmeṣanimeṣābhyāṃ jagataḥ pralayodayau"* (By whose opening and closing of eyes the world rises and dissolves.)

This "opening and closing of eyes" is the cosmic *Spanda*. It is the initial, subtle vibration that, through successive differentiations, eventually gives rise to the entire manifest universe. It's a continuous, eternal throb, not a one-time event. The universe is not separate from Śiva-Śakti; it is a direct emanation, a living vibration of the Absolute.

Singular Event vs. Eternal Vibration

When cosmologists speak of the Big Bang, they typically describe a **singular event** approximately 13.8 billion years ago. From an infinitely dense, hot point, space and time began to expand, giving birth to matter, energy, and the fundamental forces. It is seen as a dramatic, one-time creation event.

The Śaiva understanding of *Spanda*, however, proposes an **eternal vibration**. The universe is not created *at* a point in time, but is constantly emerging *from* the timeless "That One." The Big Bang, from this perspective, is not an explosion *of* something *into* nothing, but an appearance *within* consciousness.

Think of a dream. You fall asleep, and suddenly an entire world of people, places, and events appears. It feels real, it has a sense of time and space, yet it is all contained within your consciousness. When you wake up, the dream world dissolves, but *you* remain.

Similarly, the cosmos is seen as a "dream" or manifestation within the infinite consciousness of Śiva-Śakti. The Big Bang is merely the most dramatic phase of this ongoing, self-contained display.

Comparison with the Standard Cosmological Model

Let's place the ancient insights alongside modern scientific understanding.

The Big Bang (Standard Model)

- **Origin:** Infinitely dense, hot singularity.
- **Time:** Began at the moment of the Big Bang.
- **Space:** Began at the moment of the Big Bang.
- **Causality:** Linear, with the Big Bang as the ultimate first cause.
- **Nature:** Primarily material, governed by physical laws.

Spanda (Śaiva Philosophy)

- **Origin:** Unmanifest, self-existent, conscious "That One."
- **Time:** Emerges from the timeless; not fundamental.
- **Space:** Emerges from the spaceless; not fundamental.
- **Causality:** Recursive; the manifestation is the self-recognition of consciousness.
- **Nature:** Primarily conscious, with matter as a secondary manifestation.

Where they converge is the idea of a **Singularity**. Both models posit a point (or state) beyond our current understanding of physics, where familiar laws break down. The difference lies like that singularity. Science describes a physical singularity. Śaivism describes a **Consciousness Singularity**.

Even in quantum physics, the concept of a "vacuum" is not truly empty. It is a bustling sea of virtual particles constantly popping in and out of existence—a quantum foam of potential. This resembles *Spanda*, the ceaseless vibration underlying all manifest reality.

Creation as Appearance, Not Production

The critical distinction in non-dual philosophy is that the universe is not "produced" or "manufactured" by Śiva as a carpenter makes a table. Instead, it **appears** in Śiva, just as a mirage appears in the desert, or a dream appears in the mind. The underlying reality (the desert, the dreamer) remains unchanged.

This concept is called **Vivarta** in Advaita Vedānta—an apparent modification without actual transformation. It's like gold appearing as jewelry; the jewelry is merely a form, but the essence is always gold. The universe is an appearance of Śiva-Śakti.

The ***Viśva-ātmaka*** (universal self) that emerges is always inseparable from its source. The ripples are not separate from the ocean; they are the ocean in a state of activity. This resolves the paradox of "creation": there is no separate "creation" from a separate "creator." There is only the continuous, self-effulgent dance of consciousness.

The Vibration You Are

We began with the deepest silence and encountered a primordial throb. This throb, whether called the Big Bang or Spanda, is the very pulse of reality. It is the continuous unfolding of the universe from a singular, conscious source.

This understanding is not just an abstract idea. It has profound implications for how you see yourself. You are not a random accident in a dead universe. You are a localized, complex expression of that very Spanda, a unique waveform in the ocean of Śiva-consciousness. The primordial vibration is not "out there" in a distant past; it is the living essence of your own being, here and now.

When you feel the throb of your heart, hear the hum of the world, or even think a thought, you are experiencing the eternal Spanda. You are witnessing the Big Bang, moment by moment, from the inside.

Chapter -2

Advaita Vedānta: The Architecture of Reality and Illusion

Imagine you are watching a movie—an epic drama unfolding on a vast screen. The characters feel real, their struggles intense, their joys palpable. You might laugh, cry, or even gasp in suspense. For the duration of the film, you are completely immersed, forgetting yourself and the theater around you. But then, the credits roll, the lights come up, and you remember: it was just a movie. The world on screen, while powerfully convincing, was an elaborate projection, a story woven from light and shadow.

Now, extend this analogy to your entire existence. What if the universe you perceive—with its myriad forms, its undeniable solidity, its triumphs and tragedies—is also a grand, magnificent projection? What if the "you" experiencing it is not merely a character in the film, but something far more fundamental, something that encompasses both the screen and the viewer?

This radical proposition lies at the heart of Advaita Vedānta, one of the most influential non-dual philosophies to emerge from ancient India. For centuries, its insights, primarily articulated by the eighth-century sage Śaṅkara, have challenged our most cherished assumptions about reality, identity, and the very nature of existence. This chapter will delve into the architecture of this profound vision, exploring its core concepts and revealing why it offers not just a philosophical framework, but a direct pathway to understanding the deepest truths of consciousness.

The Unfolding of Non-Duality

Advaita, meaning "not two," posits a singular, ultimate reality. Everything we perceive as distinct—every object, every thought, every individual self—is, at its core, a manifestation or appearance of this one reality. It's a philosophy that doesn't just ask us to believe in oneness; it provides a systematic method for realizing it. This realization isn't an intellectual exercise; it's a profound shift in perspective that transforms our experience of life.

Brahman: The Unspeakable Infinite

At the apex of Advaita Vedānta stands Brahman—the ultimate, unconditioned, and all-pervading reality. It is the ground of all being, the source from which everything arises and into which everything dissolves. Yet, Brahman is not a "thing" in the way we understand objects. It cannot be described by any qualities, for to do so would limit it. It is beyond space, beyond time, beyond cause and effect.

The Upaniṣads, the foundational texts of Vedānta, refer to Brahman through negation (***neti neti—"not this, not*** *this*") because any positive description would diminish its boundlessness. It is pure existence (Sat), pure consciousness (Cit), and pure bliss (Ānanda). These are not attributes of Brahman, but rather its very essence.

In modern cosmology, we grapple with similar concepts when we talk about the initial singularity of the Big Bang—a point of infinite density and temperature from which the universe emerged. While not identical, the singularity represents a boundary condition, a state beyond our current descriptive power, much like Nirguṇa Brahman (Brahman without qualities). Theoretical physicists explore concepts like the "zero-point energy" or the "quantum foam" of the vacuum, hinting at a dynamic, vibrant substratum underlying apparent emptiness. These are faint echoes of a quest to understand an unmanifest potentiality, akin to Brahman.

The ***Taittirīya Upaniṣad*** states: "***That from which these beings are born, by which they live, into which they enter after death—that is Brahman.***" This isn't a creator god in the conventional sense, but the very fabric of existence itself.

Māyā: The Cosmic Veiling

If Brahman is the one ultimate reality, then what explains the incredibly diverse, seemingly solid world we inhabit? This is where the concept of Māyā enters the picture. Māyā is not an illusion in the sense of something nonxistent; rather, it's a power, a mysterious energy that conceals Brahman and projects the appearance of a pluralistic world.

Think of Māyā as a cosmic projector. Brahman is the screen, unblemished and unchanging. Māyā is the power that generates the movie, with all its vivid characters, landscapes, and storylines, appearing on that screen. The screen itself isn't affected by the drama, yet without it, no movic could appear.

Māyā has two primary functions:

1. ***Avarana Śakti (Veiling Power):*** It conceals the true nature of Brahman, making us forget the underlying unity.
2. ***Vikṣepa Śakti (Projecting Power):*** It projects the illusion of a diverse world of names and forms (nāma-rūpa), leading us to believe in its independent reality.

Māyā is often described as anirvacanīya, meaning "indescribable" or "neither real nor unreal." It cannot be called real because it disappears upon the dawn of true knowledge (like the movie vanishing when the projector is turned off). Yet, it cannot be called unreal because it has a pragmatic reality; we experience its effects every moment.

Philosophically, Māyā explains how the formless appears as form, how the one appears as many. It's the inherent creative potency of the Absolute. In a mathematical sense, one might consider Māyā as the operator or transformation function that takes the undifferentiated potential of Brahman and generates the observable universe with all its complex structures and laws. It's the "algorithm" of reality's appearance.

Vivarta: Appearance Without Transformation

Central to understanding Māyā is the concept of Vivarta, or apparent transformation. This is crucial for maintaining the non-dual nature of Brahman. Unlike parinama (actual transformation, like milk turning into yogurt), vivarta means that the cause remains unchanged while its effect appears.

The classic example is the rope appearing as a snake in dim light. The rope itself has not become a snake; it remains a rope. The snake is merely an appearance, a superimposition (adhyāsa) due to insufficient light and a conditioned mind. When the light comes, the snake vanishes, and the rope is revealed to have been there all along. The rope does not undergo any actual change or modification.

Similarly, Brahman does not actually transform into the world. The world is an appearance of Brahman, just as the snake is an appearance of the rope. Brahman remains pure, untouched, and ever-present, even as the universe seems to manifest from it. This maintains the absolute non-duality of Brahman—it is not divided or altered by its apparent manifestations. This idea is profound because it means the "creation" of the universe does not diminish or change the source. It's a bit like a holographic projection, where the entire image is contained in every part of the source, and the projection doesn't alter the source itself.

Adhyāsa: The Cosmic Error

Adhyāsa is the psychological counterpart to Māyā and Vivarta. It refers to superimposition—the erroneous attribution of the properties of one thing to another. In essence, it's the human tendency to mistake the apparent for the real, the conditioned for the unconditioned.

The rope-snake analogy is the perfect illustration. Our perception of a snake is superimposed onto the rope. The attributes of a snake (danger, movement, form) are mistakenly ascribed to the rope. This happens due to ignorance (avidyā).

On a cosmic scale, Adhyāsa is the fundamental error of identifying the true Self (Ātman)—which is none other than Brahman—with the limited, changing body-mind complex. We superimpose "I-ness" and "mine-ness" onto our physical bodies, our thoughts, our emotions, our roles, and our possessions. This superimposition creates the illusion of a separate individual, a jīva, distinct from the whole. It's the root cause of all suffering, as we cling to what is impermanent and mistake it for our true, eternal nature.

The Bṛhadāraṇyaka Upaniṣad declares: "Aham Brahmāsmi" (I am Brahman). This isn't an arrogant claim of personal divinity, but a direct statement refuting Adhyāsa, affirming that the individual Self is not separate from the Absolute. The entire spiritual journey in Advaita is the systematic removal of these superimpositions until the underlying reality of Brahman-Ātman is realized.

The Three States of Consciousness: A Daily Proof

Advaita Vedānta doesn't just present abstract philosophical concepts; it grounds its teachings in our everyday cxpcrience. Śaṅkara meticulously analyzed the three common states of consciousness we all traverse daily, demonstrating how they reveal the nature of reality and illusion.

1. Jāgrat (Waking State)

This is the state we usually consider "real." In the jāgrat state, we perceive a world of diverse objects through our senses. We interact with people, places, and things. We experience cause and effect, time, and space. Our ego, our sense of "I" as a distinct individual, is fully operational. The world appears external, objective, and independently existing.

From the Advaitic perspective, while pragmatically real for our daily interactions, the waking state is not ultimately real in the absolute sense. Its reality is conditional, dependent on the mind and senses. Just as the movie on the screen is real within the context of the film, the waking world is real within its own frame of reference.

2. Svapna (Dream State)

When we enter the svapna state, the world around us dissolves. Our senses are disengaged from external objects. Yet, a new world arises, seemingly just as real, vivid, and often emotionally charged as the waking world. In a dream, we can fly, meet fantastical creatures, or revisit long-lost friends. The dream-self experiences fear, joy, and sorrow.

Upon waking, we recognize the dream world was a creation of our own mind, lacking objective reality. The dream objects had no independent existence outside our consciousness. The dream "you" was not your waking "you." This state offers a powerful analogy for Māyā: the dream world is projected by the individual mind, just as the waking world is ultimately projected by the cosmic Māyā. Both are temporary, mind-dependent appearances.

3. Suṣupti (Deep Sleep State)

The suṣupti state is the most profound and mysterious. In deep, dreamless sleep, there are no objects of perception, no thoughts, no emotions, no "I" as a distinct entity. We experience a state of pure, undifferentiated bliss and peace. Upon waking, we often say, "I slept soundly; I knew nothing."

This "knowing nothing" is crucial. It's not a void or an annihilation of consciousness. Rather, it's a state where the individual mind (ego, intellect, senses) has temporarily dissolved, revealing a pristine, objectless consciousness. In deep sleep, the veiling power of Māyā (Avarana Śakti) is dominant, concealing the world and the individual "I," but without any projection. There is pure awareness, without any content. This state offers a glimpse into the nature of

Brahman—undifferentiated, blissful consciousness, untouched by the phenomenal world.

The Mandukya Upanishad, a text entirely dedicated to these states, points to a fourth state, Turiya, which transcends and underlies all three. Turiya is not a fourth state in sequence, but the foundational consciousness that illuminates all states. It is the unblinking awareness that observes waking, dreams, and deep sleep. This Turiya is identical to Brahman, our true Self.

Tat Tvam Asi: The Ontological Equation

"Tat Tvam Asi" (Thou Art That) is one of the Mahāvākyas, the "Great Sayings" of the Upaniṣads. This phrase, delivered by the sage Uddālaka to his son Śvetaketu in the Chāndogya Upaniṣad, is not a moral commandment or a spiritual aspiration. It is a direct statement of ontological identity—an equation revealing the true nature of reality.

- ***Tat ("That"): Refers to Brahman, the ultimate, all-pervading, unconditioned reality, the source and substratum of all existence.***
- ***Tvam ("Thou"): Refers to Ātman, the individual Self, the innermost essence of who you are, stripped of all superimpositions.***
- ***Asi ("Art"): Signifies the absolute, non-dual identity between "That" and "Thou."***

The brilliance of Śaṅkara's Advaita is how he interprets this identity. It's not that your small, individual ego becomes Brahman, or that you merge with some external cosmic entity. Rather, "Tat Tvam Asi" reveals that your true Self already is Brahman. The apparent separation was an illusion born of Māyā and Adhyāsa.

This is where the limits of language become profoundly evident. **"Thou Art That"** uses words, but it points to a reality beyond linguistic description. It's an apophatic knowing, a knowing by negation—not by asserting what Brahman is, but by eliminating what it is not. By systematically negating all limited identifiers (body, mind, emotions, roles), what remains is That which cannot be negated—pure, unbounded consciousness.

In a sense, "**Tat Tvam Asi**" is the ultimate unification theory of consciousness and reality. It's like a mathematical equation that simplifies complex variables to reveal a fundamental identity. If one were to assign a symbol to the ultimate, unmanifest potential of the universe (Brahman) and another to the deepest core of individual awareness (Ātman), this phrase asserts their absolute equivalence. It's the ***"$E=mc^2$"*** of metaphysics, equating the seemingly disparate aspects of reality into a singular truth.

The Dance of Paradox and Revelation

Advaita Vedānta, with its intricate dance between reality and illusion, Brahman and Māyā, offers a profound lens through which to view not just ancient wisdom, but also the cutting edge of modern science. The paradox of a universe that seems real but is ultimately an appearance resonates with questions in quantum physics about the observer effect and the nature of reality at its most fundamental level.

Our quest in "Shiva and Singularity" is to bridge these realms. Shiva, as the cosmic dancer, symbolises the constant creation and dissolution, the energetic pulsation of the universe—the very Māyā and Vivarta that project the world. The singularity, in physics, represents the boundary where our known laws break down, much like the point where Māyā conceals Brahman, hinting at an underlying reality beyond our current comprehension.

Ultimately, Advaita Vedānta is not a system of beliefs to be intellectually grasped, but a framework for direct experience. It challenges us to look beyond the surface, to question our deepest assumptions, and to recognise that the ground of all being is not external, but lies at the very core of who and what we truly are. The journey isn't about becoming something new, but about realizing what has always been.

The next time you gaze at the night sky, or feel the warmth of the sun on your skin, ask yourself: Is this objective reality, or a magnificent projection? Is the "I" experiencing it a separate entity, or a localized awareness of the boundless That? The answer, according to Advaita, lies not in words, but in the silent recognition of your own essential nature. The movie is playing, but you are also the screen.

Chapter 3

Śaivāgama: The Blueprint of Emanation and Reabsorption

If you strike a silent tuning fork and hold it near another of the same frequency, the second fork will begin to sing. This is resonance. But what if the entire universe is not just the music, but the instrument, the player, and the listener all at once?

In the previous chapter, we explored Advaita Vedānta's vision of the world as an illusion—a "rope mistaken for a snake." While that perspective offers profound liberation, it often leaves the seeker wondering: If the world is an illusion, why is it so beautiful, so structured, and so convincingly real?

Śaivāgama, particularly the Trika system of Kashmir, provides the answer. It suggests that the universe is not a mistake or a dream to be discarded, but an intentional "emanation" of Shiva's own light. Here, reality is not a "magic trick," but a systematic descent of consciousness into matter.

This chapter explores the architectural blueprint of existence. We will move from the mathematical elegance of the 36 Tattvas to the five cosmic acts of Shiva, ultimately discovering why this "world-affirming" vision is the essential bridge between the ancient spirit and modern science.

The 36 Tattvas: The Ladder of Light

In physics, we describe the universe by breaking it down into fundamental particles and forces. We move from the macroscopic world of galaxies down to molecules, atoms, and eventually quantum fields. Śaivāgama performs a similar "reduction," but it begins with Consciousness rather than matter.

These levels of reality are called Tattvas, a Sanskrit word meaning "thatness" or "principle." While Vedānta typically speaks of 24 principles of nature, the Śaiva tradition expands this to 36, mapping the precise stages where the Infinite Singular (Shiva) becomes the Finite Many (the individual).

The Pure Tattvas: The State of Unity

The first five Tattvas represent the "Pure Way" (Śuddha-adhvan). At this level, consciousness is still aware of its own infinite nature. It is like a mirror that is beginning to realize it can reflect things, but it hasn't yet focused on a specific image.

- *Shiva Tattva:* Pure, undifferentiated light (Prakāśa). This is the mathematical equivalent of the "Singularity" before the Big Bang—infinite potential with zero dimensions.
- *Śakti Tattva:* The dynamic energy of Shiva (Vimarśa). If Shiva is the fire, Śakti is the heat. In cosmology, this is the "inflationary" potential—the inherent "urge" to expand.

As we descend through Sadāśiva, Īśvara, and Śuddha-vidyā Tattvas, the "I" and the "This" (the universe) begin to balance. It is the birth of subjectivity and objectivity within a single field of awareness.

The Veiling: Māyā and the Five Sheaths

The most fascinating part of this blueprint occurs at the sixth Tattva: Māyā. Unlike the Vedāntic view where Māyā is a deceptive illusion, in Śaivāgama, Māyā is a "limitation."

To manifest a specific universe, the Infinite must temporarily "forget" its infinity. To experience a sunset, you must have a location in space and a moment in time. Shiva uses Māyā to create five "sheaths" (Kañcukas) that restrict his power:

1. ***Kāla: Limits eternity into Time.***
2. ***Niyati: Limits omnipresence into Space and Causality.***
3. ***Rāga: Limits fullness into Desire (the feeling of "I want").***
4. ***Vidyā: Limits omniscience into Limited Knowledge.***
5. ***Kalā: Limits omnipotence into Limited Action.***

Mathematically, this is a process of Symmetry Breaking. In the early universe, the fundamental forces (gravity, electromagnetism, nuclear forces) were once a single unified force. As the universe cooled, this symmetry broke into the distinct laws we see today. The Kañcukas are the metaphysical version of symmetry breaking—transforming the Unified Field into the fragmented world of physics.

Pañcakṛtya: The Five Acts of Cosmic Dance

If the Tattvas are the "map," the Pañcakṛtya is the "motion." In Śaivism, God is not a retired creator who made the world and sat back. Reality is a continuous, high-frequency performance. Shiva is defined by five ongoing acts:

1. Sṛṣṭi (Emanation)

This is the "out-pouring." It is not just the Big Bang billions of years ago, but the constant flow of thoughts from your mind and particles from the vacuum. It is the "Plus" in the equation of existence.

2. Sthiti (Maintenance)

The force of inertia and balance. It is the reason the chair you sit on doesn't dissolve into subatomic mist instantly. It is the stability of the laws of physics (F=ma) that allows life to thrive.

3. Saṁhāra (Reabsorption)

Commonly translated as "destruction," but more accurately "withdrawal." When you finish a thought, it returns to the silence of your mind. When a star dies, its matter is recycled. Everything that expands must eventually contract.

4. Tirobhāva (Concealment)

This is the "Cosmic Hide-and-Seek." For the play to be interesting, the Actor must forget he is acting. This is the force that makes the world feel solid and the Self feel small and separate.

5. Anugraha (Grace/Revelation)

The moment of "Aha!" It is the force of evolution and awakening. It is when the limited individual suddenly realizes, I am not just the wave; I am the Ocean. In physics, this is like the "Observation" that collapses the wave function into a localized reality.

Kulamārga vs. Advaita Vedānta

To Escape or To Embrace?

A central tension in Indian philosophy is between the "Exclusive" and the "Inclusive" paths.

Advaita Vedānta is often Exclusive (Nivṛtti). It teaches that because the world is a superimposition on Brahman, we must transcend the world to find the Truth. The metaphor is "Neti, Neti" (Not this, Not this). It is a path of subtraction.

Śaivāgama (the Kulamārga or Trika path) is Inclusive (Pravṛtti). It teaches that because the world is an emanation of Shiva, the world itself is divine. The chair, the atom, the galaxy, and the human body are all "Shiva-stuff." The metaphor is "Iti, Iti" (This too, is That).

"The world is not a prison to escape, but a poem written by the Divine in the ink of its own Being."

For the modern reader, this is a vital distinction. It means that science and spirituality are not enemies. If the physical world is "Shiva in form," then studying the laws of thermodynamics or the calculus of orbits is actually a form of worship—a way of mapping the mind of the Absolute.

The Mathematical Echo: Entropy and Information

There is a striking mathematical parallel between Śaiva reabsorption (Saṁhāra) and the laws of Information Theory. In physics, Entropy is the measure of disorder. As the universe ages, entropy increases. However, some physicists argue that "Information" is never lost.

In the Śaiva view, when the universe is reabsorbed, it doesn't become "nothing." It returns to a state of Seed

Potential (Bīja). Just as a complex computer program can be compressed into a single string of binary code, the entire complexity of the 36 Tattvas is compressed back into the Singularity of Shiva.

The equation of the universe in this system is not $0 + 1 = 1$. It is more like

1 = Infinity, where the "One" (Shiva) and the "Infinite" (the universe) are different states of the same value. The descent through the Tattvas is an increase in "Information Density" and a decrease in "Freedom." The spiritual path is the reversal of this entropy—returning to the state of Maximum Freedom.

The Architecture of You

The blueprint of Śaivāgama matters because it changes your "location" in the universe. You are not a random biological accident on a pale blue dot. You are a localized "node" where the 36 Tattvas have reached a level of complexity that allows the universe to look back at itself.

When you feel limited by time (Kāla) or space (Niyati), remember that these are not walls—they are the "costume" you have put on to play the human game. You are the Singularity masquerading as a person.

The architecture of reality is not built of bricks and mortar, but of light and vibration. As we move into the next chapter, we will look at how this vibration takes form in the most famous symbol of the non-dual vision: the dance of Natarāja, where the laws of physics and the ecstasy of the soul become one.

Chapter 4

Quantum Weirdness and the Śiva State

QUANTUM WEIRDENA STATE

Imagine a coin spinning on a tabletop. While it spins, it is neither "heads" nor "tails." It is a blurred shimmer, a singular state that holds the potential for both outcomes simultaneously. Only when you slap your hand down to stop it does it "become" one or the other.

In the macro world of clocks and cars, we assume things have a fixed reality regardless of whether we are looking at them. But in the subatomic basement of the universe, the coin never stops spinning until an observer enters the room. This is the "weirdness" of quantum mechanics—a field of study that has spent a century proving that the foundation of the physical world is not physical at all.

This chapter explores the startling convergence between quantum physics and the ancient non-dual state of Śiva. We will examine how the "superposition" of particles mirrors the infinite potential of Śakti, how the act of measurement echoes the Vedic concept of Dṛṣṭi-Śṛṣṭi Vāda, and why the universe appears to be a "participatory" reality that requires consciousness to exist.

Understanding this bridge matters because it shifts us from being victims of a mechanical universe to being co-creators of a resonant one.

Superposition: Śakti as Infinite Potential

In classical physics, an object occupies one place at one time. In quantum mechanics, a particle exists in a "superposition"—a mathematical state where it is essentially in all possible places at once. This is described by the Schrödinger Wave Equation:

Psi(x, t)

> This symbol, Psi (Psi), represents the "wave function." It is not a physical wave like water; it is a wave of probability. It is a mathematical map of what could happen.

In the language of the Śaivāgama, this is the very definition of Śakti. Before the universe manifests into distinct forms, it exists as Parāśakti—the supreme power of absolute potentiality. Just as the quantum wave function contains every possible position of an atom, Śakti contains every possible galaxy, thought, and life form within her "womb" of light.

This state is called Avyakta in Sanskrit—the unmanifest. It is a state of "Super-position" because it is not "nothing"; it is "everything, not yet chosen." It is the cosmic "Hum" before the first note of the song is struck.

The Measurement Problem: Dṛṣṭi-Śṛṣṭi Vāda

The most haunting question in physics is this: How does the "blurred" wave of probability become a "solid" particle? What causes the wave function to collapse?

Experimental data shows that the mere act of observation forces the universe to make a choice. This is known as the "Measurement Problem." Until a conscious observer (or a measuring device representing one) interacts with the system, the particle remains a ghost of possibilities.

This mirrors the philosophical doctrine of Dṛṣṭi-Śṛṣṭi Vāda—the "theory of creation through perception." This ancient Vedic insight suggests that "to be is to be perceived." The world is not sitting "out there" waiting for us to find it; the world is "appearing here" because we are looking at it.

- ***Dṛṣṭi: The gaze or consciousness.***
- ***Śṛṣṭi: The manifestation or creation.***

In the Śiva state, the Observer and the Observed are a single circuit. When you look at a star, the photons hitting your retina are the final step in a cosmic handshake. Modern physics calls this the "Participatory Universe." As physicist John Wheeler famously noted, the universe does not exist "out there" independent of us; we are part of the process of its "becoming."

Entanglement: The Non-Local Unity of Shiva

If you take two subatomic particles, let them interact, and then send them to opposite ends of the galaxy, they remain "entangled." If you change the spin of one, the other changes instantaneously—faster than the speed of light.

Einstein called this ***"spooky action at a distance***." It violates the law of locality, which says that things can only be affected by their immediate surroundings. Entanglement proves that at a fundamental level, the separation between "here" and "there" is an illusion.

This is the scientific signature of Advaita (Non-duality). In the non-dual vision, the entire universe is a single, seamless fabric of consciousness. The Vedantic tradition uses the metaphor of "Indra's Net"—a vast cosmic web where every knot contains a jewel that reflects every other jewel in the net.

Mathematically, entanglement suggests that the "state vector" of the universe cannot be separated into individual parts. There are no "parts," only a whole that appears as parts. This is the "Śiva State"—the realization that the Singularity did not happen once, long ago. The Singularity is the current and constant underlying reality of every atom.

The Ṛg Veda (1.164.46) captures this perfectly:

"Ekaṃ sad viprā bahudhā vadanti"(Truth is One, though the wise call it by many names.)

Physics simply adds: "Reality is One, though the instruments measure it as many particles."

Why Physics Silently Assumes Consciousness

For decades, science tried to build a model of the universe that didn't need "mind." They wanted a universe of cold marble and clockwork. However, quantum mechanics has made that impossible.

The "Wave-Particle Duality" shows that matter responds to how we ask it questions. If we set up an experiment to look for waves, we see waves. If we look for particles, we see particles. The "matter" is essentially a mirror reflecting the intent of the seeker.

This leads us to the inevitable conclusion: Consciousness is not a byproduct of matter; it is the substrate of matter. In mathematics, we use "Complex Numbers" (involving the imaginary unit i, where i^2 = -1) to describe quantum states. These numbers are necessary to make the equations work, even though they represent values that don't exist in the "real" physical world. Similarly, Consciousness is the "Imaginary" factor—the invisible dimension—that makes the physical equations of the universe possible.

Without the "I" of the observer, the "It" of the universe remains a mathematical abstraction. This is the "Śiva-Śakti" union. Śiva is the silent, witnessing Awareness (the Observer), and Śakti is the dynamic, vibrating energy (the

Observed). Without Śiva, Śakti has no direction. Without Śakti, Śiva has no expression.

The Apophatic Limit: Beyond the Equation

Despite the precision of our mathematics, there is a point where physics falls silent. We can calculate the probability of where an electron will be, but we can never say why it chose to appear there.

This is the boundary of "Apophatic Knowing"—knowing by realizing what cannot be known. The Kena Upaniṣad states:

"He who thinks he knows, knows not. He who knows that he knows not, truly knows."

In science, this is represented by Heisenberg's Uncertainty Principle. There is a fundamental limit to what can be measured. This "Uncertainty" is not a failure of our technology; it is a feature of reality. It is the "Singularity" hiding in every point of space—a reminder that the source of the universe is always beyond the reach of language and measurement.

Awakening the Observer

Quantum physics does not just tell us about atoms; it tells us about ourselves. It tells us that we are not insignificant specks in a vast, indifferent void. We are the "Measurement" that brings the world into focus.

The "Śiva State" is the recognition of this power. It is the shift from being a "character in a movie" to being the "Light in the Projector." When you realize that your own awareness is the same field that collapses the wave functions of distant stars, you stop fearing the world and start resonating with it.

If the universe is an entangled, participatory dance of potential, then every thought you think and every gaze you cast is an act of creation. You are the singularity experiencing itself through the lens of a human life.

The question is no longer "What is the universe?" but "Who is the one asking?"

Chapter 5

Cosmology's Singularity and the Formless Śiva

Imagine tracing a river upstream, past tributaries, rapids, and ancient forests, until you reach its source. You expect a spring, a lake, or a melting glacier. But what if, instead, you find a point where the river simply stops—a boundary beyond which the very concept of "river" ceases to make sense?

This is the perplexing situation cosmologists face when they peer back in time to the very beginning of our universe. They encounter a singularity—a moment when all the known laws of physics break down, where space and time as we understand them dissolve. It's a boundary that science, by its very nature, cannot cross.

This chapter delves into the scientific mystery of the Big Bang singularity and finds its profound echo in the ancient wisdom of the formless Śiva. We will explore how yogic cosmology's Bindu aligns with physics' uncrossable point, how black holes offer a glimpse into cosmic dissolution (Laya), and why, at the edge of the quantifiable, metaphysics becomes the essential guide.

This journey matters because it reveals the inherent limitations of purely material understanding and points towards a reality that transcends measurement—a reality that the ancient sages knew intimately.

The Big Bang Singularity: Where Equations Fail

Modern cosmology, built on Einstein's theory of General Relativity, paints a stunning picture of the universe's evolution. It describes an expanding cosmos that was once incredibly hot and dense. Tracing this expansion backward, we arrive at a theoretical point of infinite density and zero volume. This is the Big Bang singularity.

At this point, our mathematical models—the very language we use to understand the universe—cease to function. Imagine trying to divide a number by zero; the answer is undefined. Similarly, at the singularity:

- ***Density: Infinite***
- ***Temperature: Infinite***
- ***Space-Time Curvature: Infinite***

This isn't just a "small gap" in our knowledge. It's a fundamental breakdown. It implies that space and time themselves, which emerged from the Big Bang, cannot meaningfully exist before it. We cannot ask "What happened before the Big Bang?" because "before" is a concept within time, and time began at the Big Bang.

Physicists refer to this as a "naked singularity," a region where the fabric of space-time is ripped apart, and all information is lost. It's a conceptual abyss where the known universe meets its unknowable source.

Bindu: The Yogic Seed-Point

In yogic and Tantric cosmology, a concept strikingly similar to the Big Bang singularity exists: the Bindu (बन्दि). Meaning "point" or "drop," the Bindu represents the unmanifest, undifferentiated source of all creation. It is the cosmic seed, the potent singularity from which the entire universe unfurls.

The Bindu is not a physical point in space; it is a metaphysical principle, a dimensionless point of pure potential. It exists prior to the distinction of form, name, space, or time.

- **Cosmic Seed:** Before creation (Sṛṣṭi), the universe resides as pure potential within the Bindu. It contains the entire blueprint, the holographic information of the cosmos, in a state of supreme compression.
- **Unity of Shiva and Shakti:** The Bindu is often depicted as the point where Shiva (pure consciousness) and Shakti (dynamic energy) are in perfect, inseparable union—a state of "non-dual equilibrium." It is the "I AM" before "I AM this."

Just as the Big Bang singularity is the point where our equations break down, the Bindu represents the state where language itself fails. It can only be pointed to, not described. It is the ultimate apophatic reality—known by its effects, but unknowable in its essence.

The Śaiva-sūtras begin with: "Caitanyam Ātmā" (Consciousness is the Self.) And implicitly, this Consciousness, in its ultimate unmanifest form, is the

Bindu—the pure, undifferentiated "I" from which all manifest reality emanates.

Black Holes: Laya in Action

If the Big Bang represents the cosmic Sṛṣṭi (emanation) from a singularity, then Black Holes represent Laya (dissolution or reabsorption) into a singularity.

A black hole is formed when a massive star collapses under its own gravity, creating a region of space-time where gravity is so intense that nothing—not even light—can escape. At the heart of every black hole lies its own singularity, a point of infinite density where matter is crushed out of existence, and the laws of physics once again cease to apply.

In a black hole:

- ***Event Horizon:*** The boundary beyond which escape is impossible. It is a one-way membrane.
- ***Singularity:*** The ultimate destination, a point of infinite curvature and density, where the familiar dimensions of space and time lose their meaning.

From a yogic perspective, a black hole is a microcosm of cosmic dissolution (Saṁhāra). It is where the manifested universe (matter, energy, space-time) is reabsorbed back into the unmanifest. Just as the Bindu is the source, the black hole's singularity is the ultimate sink, swallowing back all that has been projected.

The parallels are striking: both the Big Bang singularity and black hole singularities are points where our scientific understanding collapses. They are "windows" into the formless, revealing the inherent impermanence of all forms.

Why Physics Cannot Cross the Singularity—But Metaphysics Can

The reason physics cannot cross the singularity is fundamental: physics deals with the phenomenal world—that which can be measured, observed, and described within the framework of space, time, matter, and energy. A singularity, by definition, is where these very frameworks break down.

It's like trying to navigate a map that suddenly has a hole in it, labeled "here be dragons." The map's language of roads and landmarks ceases to apply.

Mathematics offers a clue: In General Relativity, the singularity is a point where certain quantities (like density and curvature) go to infinity. In a purely mathematical sense, infinity is not a number; it's a concept of boundless magnitude. When our equations yield infinity, it often signals that we have reached the limit of that particular model, or that we are describing a transition to a different order of reality.

Metaphysics, however, is designed precisely for this boundary. It asks questions that transcend the empirical: "What is ultimate reality?", "What lies beyond sensory perception?", "What is consciousness?" Where physics hits a wall, metaphysics offers a lens.

- ***The Formless Śiva:*** In Śaivism, Śiva is often depicted as Nirguṇa (without attributes) and Akala (formless). He is the ultimate, unmanifest reality that precedes and encompasses all forms. The Big Bang singularity and the black hole singularity are, in this view, temporary "gateways" back to the formless Śiva. They are cosmic pauses, where the manifest withdraws back into the unmanifest potential.
- ***Transcendent Consciousness:*** The Upaniṣads assert that the ultimate reality is consciousness, Brahman. This consciousness is not located in space or in time; it is that by which space and time are known. Therefore, consciousness can "cross" the singularity because it is prior to the very dimensions that define the singularity.

The Muṇḍaka Upaniṣad speaks of Brahman as: "*Adṛśyam, agrāhyam, avarṇam, acakṣuḥ-śrotram, tad-apāṇipādam, nityam, vibhum, sarva-gataṁ, susūkṣmaṁ, tad-avyayaṁ yad bhūta-yonim paripaśyanti dhīrāḥ.*" (Invisible, incomprehensible, without lineage, without eyes and ears, without hands and feet, eternal, all-pervading, omnipresent, exceedingly subtle; that imperishable is what the wise perceive as the source of all beings.)

This describes a reality—a formless Śiva—that perfectly fits what lies beyond the singularity.

The Singularity Within

The convergence of cosmology's singularity and Śiva's formless state is more than an intellectual curiosity; it's a profound invitation. It suggests that the ultimate truth of the universe is not found by building bigger telescopes or more powerful particle accelerators (though these are invaluable tools). It is found by turning inward, by exploring the nature of the observer.

The singularity is not just a point far back in time or deep in space; it is the silent, dimensionless core of your own being. It is the unmanifest potential from which your thoughts, emotions, and perceptions arise. It is the formless consciousness that underpins all form.

To understand the Big Bang singularity is to glimpse the face of the formless Śiva. It is to recognize that at the absolute boundary of the knowable, the universe reveals its true, mystical nature: boundless, eternal, and intimately present.

Chapter-6

The Holographic Universe and the Net of Śiva

If you were to take a common photograph of an apple and cut it in half, you would find that one half contains the top of the apple and the other contains the bottom. But if you take a holographic plate of that same apple and shatter it into a thousand pieces, a startling phenomenon occurs. When you shine a laser through any single shard, you do not see a fragment of the fruit; you see the entire apple, perfectly intact, albeit smaller.

In a hologram, the whole is not just made of parts; the whole is present in every part.

This paradox is no longer confined to the laboratory or the realm of science fiction. It has become a leading contender for the actual mathematical description of our universe. Modern physics increasingly suggests that our three-dimensional reality—the world of height, width, and depth—might be a projection of information stored on a distant, two-dimensional surface.

This chapter explores the profound convergence between the Holographic Principle of modern cosmology and the ancient Vedic metaphor of Indra's Net. We will examine how the "Viśvarūpa" or Universal Form represents the ultimate holographic realization, and why shifting our view of reality from a "container" to a "reflection" changes everything about how we inhabit this world.

The Holographic Principle: Information on the Edge

For decades, physicists believed that the "stuff" of the universe was matter and energy. However, through the study of black holes, a new primary currency has emerged: Information.

In the 1990s, Leonard Susskind and Gerard 't Hooft proposed the Holographic Principle. They realized that the amount of "information" inside a volume of space—say, a room—is not determined by the volume of the room, but by the surface area of the walls surrounding it.

Mathematically, this is expressed through the AdS/CFT correspondence. Without getting lost in the jargon, this correspondence suggests that a theory of gravity in a certain number of dimensions (Anti-de Sitter space) is exactly equivalent to a quantum theory without gravity in one fewer dimension (Conformal Field Theory).

In simpler terms: The 3D world we touch and feel may be a "physical" projection of data encoded on a 2D boundary. If the universe has a "limit" or a boundary, everything happening inside it is merely a reflection of the information on that boundary.

As the Atharva Veda (10.8.29) cryptically suggests:

"The full comes out of the full; taking the full from the full, the full itself remains."

This is the essence of a hologram—you cannot diminish the "Whole" by dividing it, because the "Whole" is the fundamental unit.

Viśvarūpa Darśana: The Universal Form as Hologram

One of the most powerful images in spiritual literature is the Viśvarūpa Darśana, famously described in the Bhagavad Gītā. When the divine reveals its true nature to the warrior Arjuna, he does not see a "large person." Instead, he sees a terrifying and beautiful totality where all times, all places, all suns, and all beings exist simultaneously within a single point.

Arjuna exclaims: "I see no beginning, middle, or end to You."

This is the spiritual equivalent of the holographic realization. In the Viśvarūpa, the "Singularity" and the "Infinite" are not separate. Every subatomic particle contains the coordinate for the entire cosmos. From a non-dual perspective, Śiva is not "in" the universe; the universe is a holographic shimmer on the surface of Śiva's consciousness.

In mathematics, we might compare this to a Fractal. A fractal is a geometric shape that is "self-similar." No matter how much you zoom in, the pattern of the whole repeats itself in the smallest detail.

If the universe is holographic, then the ancient axiom "As above, so below" is not just poetry—it is a geometric fact. The structure of the human brain mirrors the structure of the cosmic web of galaxies. The "Singularity" of the Big Bang is not an event in the past; it is the "inner boundary" of every moment.

Indra's Net: The Cosmological Web

Long before modern string theory or quantum entanglement, the Avatamsaka Sutra described a vision of the cosmos known as Indra's Nct.

Imagine a vast net that stretches infinitely in all directions. At every intersection of the threads, there is a single, highly polished jewel. Because the jewels are so clear, each individual jewel reflects every other jewel in the net—all infinite millions of them. Not only that, but each jewel also reflects the reflections of all the other jewels, ad infinitum.

This is a perfect metaphor for Non-local Unity.

- ***The Threads***: Represent the "entanglement" or the laws of physics that connect all points in space-time.
- ***The Jewels:*** Represent individual entities—atoms, people, stars.
- ***The Reflection:*** Represents the truth that no object has an "independent" existence.

In physics, we see this through Quantum Entanglement. When two particles are entangled, their "information" is shared. A change in one is reflected in the other, regardless of distance. Indra's Net suggests that the entire universe is in a state of total entanglement.

The Ṛg Veda (6.47.18) declares:

"Rūpaṃ rūpaṃ maghavā bobhavīti"

(The Lord moves in many forms by his mysterious powers.)

In the context of the net, this means the "One Light" of Śiva is what is being reflected in every jewel. The jewels are many, but the Light is one.

Reality as Reflection, Not Container

The greatest shift this chapter demands of you is to stop seeing the universe as a "container."

Most of us think of space as a big, empty box and ourselves as little marbles rattling around inside it. But the holographic view—and the Śiva-vision—suggests that space is not a container at all. Space is a property of consciousness.

If you are watching a movie, the "depth" of the landscape on the screen is an illusion created by the arrangement of pixels. There is no actual distance between the mountain in the background and the hero in the foreground; they are both equally "on the screen."

Similarly, the distance between you and a star is a holographic "depth" projected within the "Screen of Śiva."

The Mathematics of the Boundless

If we look at the equation for the entropy of a black hole (the Bekenstein-Hawking formula):

$$S_{BH} = \frac{kA}{4\ell_P^2}$$

Here, S (Entropy/Information) is proportional to A (Area), not Volume. This was the first mathematical hint that the "reality" of a 3D object is actually stored on its 2D surface.

In spiritual practice, this leads to Apophatic Knowing. If the world is a reflection, you cannot find the "Source" by traveling further into the reflection. You cannot find the projector by running toward the movie screen. To find the source, you must turn 180 degrees away from the reflection and look at the "Light" that is making the projection possible.

Integration: The Singularity is the Screen

We began this book by looking at the Singularity as a point of origin. We now see that the Singularity is more like the "Projector Lens."

The "Big Bang" is the moment the light hit the holographic plate. The "36 Tattvas" we discussed in Part I are the layers of the hologram, each adding a new level of "density" and "depth" to the projection.

When we say "Shiva and Singularity," we are talking about the "Substrate." Just as the silver on the back of a mirror allows it to reflect the world without the mirror itself becoming the world, Śiva is the "Absolute Mirror."

Living in the Light

If the universe is holographic, then you are not a "part" of the universe. You are the universe, localized at a specific "jewel" in the net.

This realization dissolves the fear of insignificance. You are not a tiny speck in a cold, vast vacuum. You are a point of view through which the Entirety is looking at itself. Every action you take sends a ripple through the entire net; every thought you think is reflected in the jewels of distant galaxies.

This matters because it restores Purpose and Participation. If the whole is in the part, then the "Sacred" is not somewhere else—it is fully present in the mundane. The "Singularity" is not 14 billion years away; it is the very fabric of your current awareness.

As you close this chapter, look at the palm of your hand. According to the holographic principle, there is enough information capacity in the surface area of your skin to describe the entire visible universe. You are, quite literally, a cosmic library.

Chapter 7

Mathematical Representation of Advaita

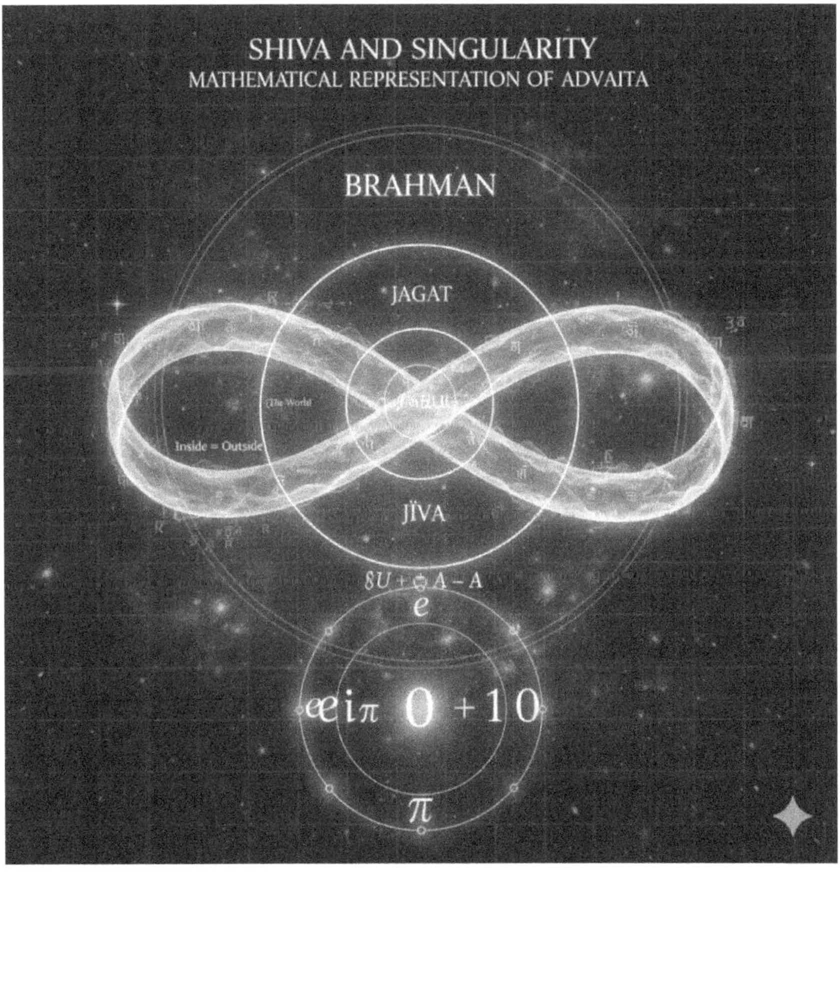

If you take a circle and divide its circumference by its diameter, you arrive at π—an infinite, non-repeating decimal that exists as a universal constant regardless of whether anyone is there to calculate it. Mathematics is often called the "language of God" because it describes truths that do not change, truths that are independent of human opinion or cultural bias.

But can equations capture the essence of the soul? Can a formula describe the non-dual reality of Śiva?

For centuries, seekers have used poetry and metaphor to describe Advaita (non-duality). In this chapter, we pivot to a different set of tools. We will explore how mathematical concepts like Set Theory, Topology, and Euler's Identity provide a rigorous architecture for spiritual intuition. We will see how the concept of Zero is not a void, but a fullness, and how the geometry of a Möbius strip reveals the secret of our own identity.

This matters because it moves spirituality out of the realm of "belief" and into the realm of "structural truth." If the universe is built on mathematical laws, and if those laws point toward oneness, then your connection to the Infinite is not a matter of faith—it is a logical necessity.

Śūnya and Pūrṇatva: The Fullness of Zero

In the West, "Zero" was long feared as a symbol of nothingness or the "abyss." However, in the Indian tradition, the word for zero is Śūnya. While it translates to "empty," its philosophical weight is closer to "limitless potential."

The Vedic vision docs not see the origin of the universe as a "void" that needs filling. Instead, it speaks of Pūrṇatva—absolute fullness. There is a famous mathematical invocation in the Isha Upaniṣad:

"Oṃ pūrṇamadaḥ pūrṇamidam pūrṇāt pūrṇamudacyate"

(That is whole, this is whole. From the whole, the whole becomes manifest.)

In modern mathematics, this mirrors the property of Infinity (\infty). If you subtract infinity from infinity, you still have infinity. If you add infinity to infinity, it remains unchanged. Śūnya is the mathematical "Singularity" that contains all numbers within itself.

Just as the number zero is the neutral point that allows the existence of both positive and negative integers, the "Śiva-Zero" is the neutral awareness that allows the world of dualities (light and dark, joy and sorrow) to appear. ***It is not "nothing"; it is the "no-thing" that supports "every-thing."***

Set Theory: The Universal and the Subset

To understand how the individual (Jīva) relates to the Absolute (Brahman), we can look to Set Theory.

In mathematics, a "Set" is a collection of objects. If we define the Universal Set (U) as Brahman, it encompasses everything that exists, has existed, or could exist. There is nothing outside of it.

- ***Brahman (The Universal Set):*** The totality of reality.
- ***Jagat (The World):*** A subset within the Universal Set.
- ***Jīva (The Individual):*** A localized subset.

The beauty of this mathematical representation is that a subset is never "not" the Universal Set. An element inside a circle is entirely supported by the space of that circle. The "Non-Dual" equation is simple:

$$\mathcal{U} \cap A = A$$

This signifies that the individual (A) has no identity whatsoever outside of the Universal Set (U). The illusion of duality arises when we draw a boundary around the subset and forget the background of the page. Advaita is simply the realization that the boundaries are "empty" sets—they have no independent existence.

Euler's Identity: The Equation of Wholeness

Many mathematicians consider Euler's Identity to be the most beautiful equation ever written:

$$e^{i\pi} + 1 = 0$$

What makes this equation remarkable is that it links five of the most important constants in mathematics: e (the base of natural logarithms), i (the imaginary unit), pi (the ratio of a circle), 1 (the unit of manifestation), and 0 (the source).

In a philosophical sense, this equation is a map of the "Singularity."

- **The Imaginary (i):** Represents the unmanifest, subtle dimensions of consciousness.
- **The Cycle (\pi):** Represents the rhythmic nature of time and creation (Samsāra).

- **The One (1):** Represents the appearance of the ego or the manifest world.
- **The Zero (0):** Represents the final dissolution into Śiva.

Euler's Identity shows that even the most complex, "imaginary" movements of the universe ultimately resolve back into the stillness of Zero. It is a mathematical proof that diversity and unity are not at odds; they are part of a single, elegant identity.

Topology: The Möbius Strip of Consciousness

One of the greatest struggles in spiritual life is the feeling that there is an "Inside" (me) and an "Outside" (the world). We feel like observers trapped in a bag of skin. To resolve this, we can turn to Topology—the study of shapes and spaces.

Consider a Möbius strip. You can create one by taking a strip of paper, giving it a single half-twist, and taping the ends together.

If you start drawing a line with a pen on the "outside" of a Möbius strip and continue long enough, you will eventually find yourself on the "inside" without ever crossing an edge. On a Möbius strip, the distinction between inside and outside is a local illusion. Globally, there is only one side.

This is the geometry of Advaita. We think our thoughts are "inside" and the stars are "outside." But in the state of Śiva-consciousness, you realize that the world is "inside" your awareness, and your awareness is "outside" in the world. As the Vedas suggest: "That which is here, is there; that which is there, is here."

By giving our perspective a "twist" through meditation or inquiry, we discover that the "Observer" and the "Observed" are two points on the same continuous surface of being.

The Apophatic Limit of Logic

While mathematics is a powerful pointer, it eventually reaches a point of Apophatic Knowing—the realization that the ultimate cannot be calculated.

In 1931, Kurt Gödel published his "Incompleteness Theorems." He proved that in any logical system complex enough to do basic arithmetic, there will always be truths that are "true" but cannot be "proven" within that system.

This was a tectonic shift in science. It meant that logic itself has a boundary. There are realities that are "Self-Evident" but beyond the reach of a step-by-step proof.

This is exactly what the sages say about the Self (Ātman). You cannot "prove" your own existence through a formula, because you are the one using the formula. You are the "Axiom" that must be assumed before any math can begin.

Consciousness is the "unproven truth" that allows all other proofs to exist.

The Final Equation

Mathematics strips away the "story" of our lives—our names, our traumas, our preferences—and reveals the skeleton of reality. It shows us that the universe is not chaotic; it is an ordered emanation of a single, non-dual principle.

The "Singularity" we speak of is not just a point in space. It is the mathematical "Origin" (0,0,0) from which every coordinate of your life is measured. Whether we use the language of Set Theory or the language of Śaivāgama, the conclusion is the same: The Many are reflections of the One.

When you look at the world through this mathematical lens, you stop being a "fragment" trying to find the "whole." You realize that you are the whole, currently expressed as a specific coordinate. The equation of your life is already solved.

Chapter 8

The Hard Problem of Consciousness: Ātman as the Field

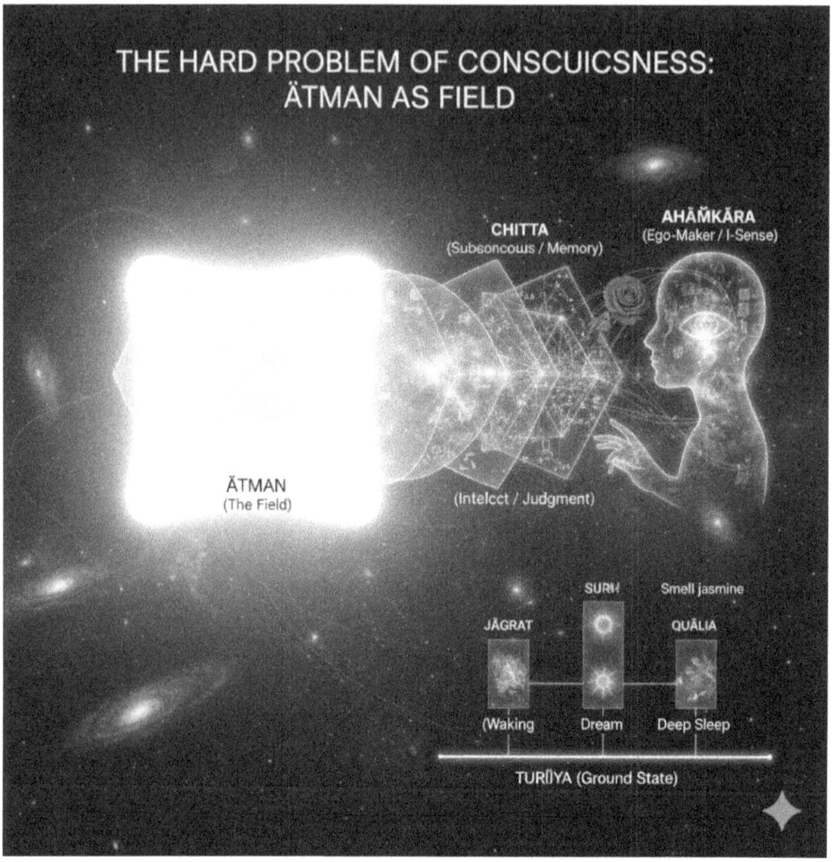

If you were to dismantle a television set, piece by piece, you would find copper wires, silicon chips, glass panels, and plastic casings. You could study the flow of electricity through the circuits and the way pixels align to create colors. Yet, no matter how deeply you scrutinized the hardware, you would never find the "story" being told on the screen. The drama, the emotion, and the meaning of the broadcast are not properties of the wires.

For decades, modern science has attempted to dismantle the human brain in search of the "viewer." We have mapped neurons, measured neurotransmitters, and tracked electrical storms across the cerebral cortex. We have found the hardware, but the "story"—the actual experience of being alive—remains elusive.

This chapter addresses what philosopher David Chalmers famously called the "Hard Problem." We will explore why the felt quality of experience, or qualia, rcfuscs to be reduced to mere biological data. By integrating the Samkhya model of the mind with modern cognitive science, we will propose that consciousness is not a byproduct of the brain, but a fundamental field—the Ātman—that precedes all physical manifestation.

This inquiry is the heart of our synthesis. If we can solve the mystery of the observer, we solve the mystery of the Singularity itself.

The Cognitive Layers: Chitta, Buddhi, and Ahaṁkāra

In the Indian philosophical tradition, the "mind" is not a single, monolithic entity. It is described as a sophisticated instrument composed of distinct functional layers, collectively known as the Antahkarana (the inner instrument). To understand the Hard Problem, we must first distinguish the instrument from the player.

1. Chitta: The Reservoir of Memory

Chitta is the subconscious mind, the vast storage bank of impressions (Samskaras) and memories. It is the raw data stream. In the language of computing, Chitta is the hard drive where every experience is logged, influencing our current reactions without our conscious intervention.

2. Buddhi: The Decisive Intellect

Buddhi is the faculty of discrimination and judgment. It is the "processor" that determines truth from falsehood. When we solve a mathematical equation or make a moral choice, Buddhi is the active agent. It is the highest function of the material mind, often mistaken for consciousness itself.

3. Ahaṁkāra: The Ego-Maker

Ahaṁkāra literally means the "I-maker." It is the psychological function that claims ownership over experience. It takes the data from Chitta and the decisions of Buddhi and says, "This is my memory; this is my choice."

While these three layers facilitate our interaction with the world, they are all considered "insentient" in Yogic philosophy. They are like the gears of a clock—moving, complex, but ultimately mechanical. The light that illuminates these gears, allowing them to be "seen," is the Ātman.

Chalmers' Hard Problem and the Knowledge Argument

Modern neuroscience excels at solving the "Easy Problems"—explaining how the brain processes light, how it triggers muscle movement, or how it categorizes sensory input. These are mechanical questions.

The "Hard Problem," however, is asking: Why is all this processing accompanied by an internal experience? Why doesn't the brain just function in the dark, like a sophisticated computer, without the "feeling" of seeing red or "feeling" the warmth of the sun?

Mary's Room: The Knowledge Argument

Consider the famous thought experiment of "Mary the Color Scientist." Mary lives in a black-and-white room and learns every physical fact about the science of color. She knows the wavelengths of light and exactly which neurons fire when someone sees "red."

One day, Mary leaves the room and sees a red rose for the first time. Does she learn something new? The answer is an intuitive "Yes." She learns what it feels like to see red. This subjective "feeling" is called a quale (plural: qualia).

Mathematically, this represents a gap in our descriptive power. If P is the set of all physical facts, and E is the set of all experiences, the Hard Problem suggests that E cannot be derived from P. There is no equation that takes "sodium ions moving across a membrane" as an input and yields "the smell of jasmine" as an output.

Why Qualia Refuse Reduction

The reason science struggles with consciousness is that science is built on objectivity—the study of things that can be measured from the outside. Consciousness, by definition, is subjectivity—the "inside" view.

In physics, we describe a particle by its mass, charge, and spin. These are external properties. But consciousness has no "outside." You cannot weigh a thought or measure the diameter of a dream.

The Bṛhadāraṇyaka Upaniṣad (3.7.23) captures this apophatic limit:

"He is the unseen Seer, the unheard Hearer, the unthought Thinker, the unknown Knower."

This implies that Consciousness is the "Ground State." In physics, the ground state is the lowest-energy state of a quantum system. In our synthesis, Ātman is the ground state of reality. It is not something the brain produces; it is the field in which the brain exists.

Turīya: The Ground State of Awareness

If we look back at the states of consciousness discussed in Chapter 2—waking, dreaming, and deep sleep—we see that they are all "contents" of awareness. They come and go. However, there is a fourth state, referred to in the Mandukya Upaniṣad as Turīya.

Turīya is not a state you "enter." It is the constant "background" that persists through all other states. It is the "silent witness" (Sakshi).

Mathematically, we can think of Turīya as the Zero-Point Field of consciousness. In quantum field theory, even in a perfect vacuum, there is a background energy that remains. Similarly, even when the mind is silent, awareness remains. This awareness is non-dual, meaning it is not divided into "me" and "not-me." It is a singular, infinite field.

Integration: Ātman and the Singularity

We began this journey by looking at the Singularity of the Big Bang—a point where space and time emerge. The Hard Problem of Consciousness leads us to a "Biological Singularity." Just as the physical singularity is the source of all matter, the Ātman is the source of all experience.

The Rig Veda (10.129) suggests that in the beginning, there was neither existence nor non-existence, only "That One" breathing breathless by its own nature. This "breathless breath" is the pulsation of pure awareness.

The synthesis we propose is this: The Singularity of physics and the Ātman of philosophy are the same "Point."

When the Singularity "vibrates" (Spanda), it appears as energy and matter. When that matter reaches a certain complexity (the human brain), it reflects the light of its source, and we call it "Consciousness."

The Hard Problem is only "hard" because we are trying to find the source of the light by looking at the shadows on the wall. When we realize we are the light, the problem dissolves.

The Viewer and the View

The quest to understand consciousness is the ultimate homecoming. It is the realization that you are not a biological accident trying to make sense of a cold universe. You are the very awareness that gives the universe its colors, its sounds, and its meaning.

The brain is not the creator of consciousness, but its finest prism. It takes the white light of the Ātman and refracts it into the rainbow of human experience—into Chitta, Buddhi, and Ahaṁkāra.

As you move through your day, remember the analogy of the television. The shows will change, the dramas will rise and fall, and the news will cycle between tragedy and triumph. But the "Screen" remains untouched. You are that screen. You are the "Singularity" in which the entire cosmos is currently playing.

Chapter 9

Śiva, Singularity, and the Unified Field

Consider the surface of a perfectly still lake at midnight. If you throw a handful of pebbles into the water, a complex interference pattern of ripples emerges. To an observer seeing only the crests of the waves, it looks like a multitude of separate, interacting objects. But to the one who sees the water itself, there is only a single, undivided liquid mass in a state of temporary agitation.

For centuries, science has studied the ripples—gravity, electromagnetism, and nuclear forces—treating them as distinct "laws" of nature. Simultaneously, spiritual traditions have studied the water—the primordial consciousness that supports all form. In this final synthesis, we find that the "Singularity" of the physicist and the "Śiva-Tattva" of the mystic are not two different things. They are the same stillness, viewed through different lenses.

This chapter explores the grand unification of consciousness and physics. We will map the "Unified Field" to the supreme state of Śiva, see how matter and time emerge as mere differentiations of that field, and ultimately realize that the "Big Bang" is not a past event, but a present, continuous vibration of the Absolte.

The Great Convergence: Parts I & II Reunited

Throughout this journey, we have navigated two seemingly separate rivers. In Part I, we waded through the philosophical bedrock of Advaita and Śaivāgama, identifying the source of reality as an infinite, non-dual awareness. In Part II, we used the lens of modern science to observe the breakdown of matter into quantum probability and the dissolution of space-time into a singularity.

Now, these rivers merge. The "Singularity" described by General Relativity is the mathematical boundary where the physical world returns to its seed-state. The "Śiva-Tattva" is the metaphysical reality of that same seed.

Science calls it the "Vacuum State" or the "Unified Field." The Upaniṣads call it Brahman. The difference is only in the language of description. One uses the quantitative language of mathematics (0, \infty, \Psi); the other uses the qualitative language of direct experience (Sat, Cit, Ānanda).

Superposition: Śakti as Infinite Potential

In theoretical physics, the "Unified Field Theory" is the holy grail. It is the attempt to find a single master equation that explains all four fundamental forces of nature. It posits that at extremely high energy levels—like those found at the moment of the Singularity—these forces lose their individual identities and merge into one.

In the hierarchy of the 36 Tattvas we explored in Chapter 3, the highest level is Śiva-Tattva. This is the state of pure, undifferentiated light (Prakāśa). It is the ultimate Unified Field.

- ***The Physicist's View:*** The field is an abstract mathematical space from which particles emerge as "excitations" or waves.
- ***The Mystic's View:*** The field is "Pure Awareness" from which thoughts and objects emerge as "vibrations" or Spanda.

As the Spanda Kārikā (1.1)

states: *"Yasyonmeṣanimeṣābhyāṃ jagataḥ pralayodayau"*

(By whose opening and closing of eyes the world rises and dissolves.)

This "opening of the eye" is the mathematical equivalent of Symmetry Breaking. When the Unified Field of Śiva begins to manifest, it "breaks" its perfect symmetry to become the diverse forces and particles of the universe.

Forces, Matter, and Space-Time as Differentiations

If the Unified Field is the ocean, then matter and energy are merely "ice cubes" made of that same water. There is no fundamental difference between the ice and the ocean, except for the rate of vibration.

In modern physics, the Higgs Field gives particles mass, effectively slowing down energy until it becomes "solid" matter. In Śaivāgama, this is the function of Māyā and the Kañcukas (the sheaths). They "contract" the infinite power of Śiva, creating the illusion of weight, boundary, and separation.

Consider the equation E=mc^2. It tells us that matter is simply condensed energy. If we go one step further into the non-dual vision, we see that energy is simply "active consciousness." Therefore:

Consciousness ------→Energy --------→ Matter

The "Forces" of nature—Gravity, Electromagnetism, and the Nuclear forces—are the different "rhythms" of Śiva's dance. They are not external laws imposed upon the universe; they are the inherent habits of the Unified Field.

Time and Causality: The Emergent Māyā-Structures

Perhaps the most persistent illusion we face is the linear flow of time—the idea of "before" and "after." In the Singularity, time as a dimension ceases to exist. Equations become "time-independent."

Advaita Vedānta refers to this as Vivarta—apparent change without actual transformation. The "Big Bang" did not happen 13.8 billion years ago in a distant past. Because the Singularity is the "Ground State," it is happening now.

Time and causality are "emergent properties." Just as the "depth" in a 2D painting is an emergent illusion created by perspective, "Time" is an emergent structure created by the mind's inability to process the totality of the Unified Field all at once.

The Yogavāsiṣṭha explains this clearly:

"Kālaḥ kalayati sarvam"

(Time is the movement of the mind itself.)

When we look through the lens of the Singularity, we see that causality is a loop. The "First Cause" (Shiva) is also the "Final Effect." In mathematics, this is represented by a Self-Referential System. The universe is a giant feedback loop where Consciousness looks at itself and perceives a "world."

The Apophatic Synthesis: Beyond the Field

Even the concept of a "Unified Field" is ultimately a pointer, not the thing itself. This is where we encounter the Apophatic Limit.

The Nāsadīya Sūkta of the Ṛg Veda (10.129) famously concludes its description of the origin of the universe by saying:

"He from whom this creation arose... whether he established it or whether he did not... he who surveys it in the highest heaven, he surely knows—or maybe he knows not!"

This is not a statement of ignorance, but a statement of the highest mathematical and spiritual honesty. At the heart of the Singularity, there is a "Godelian Incompleteness." The system cannot fully describe itself from within itself.

To "know" Śiva is not to have information about Śiva. It is to be the Field. It is to move from the "Equations" of Part II to the "Experience" of Part I.

The Singularity of the Heart

We began this book with a question: How do we reconcile the cold, mathematical singularity of the Big Bang with the warm, living presence of the Divine?

The answer lies in the realization that there is only one "Place" and one "Time." The Singularity is not a point in the sky; it is the "Point" (Bindu) in your own heart. The Unified Field is not an abstraction in a physics textbook; it is the very Awareness that is currently reading these words.

Śiva and Singularity are two names for the same Silence. One name satisfies the mind's hunger for logic; the other name satisfies the soul's hunger for belonging. When the two are synthesized, the "World" stops being a place of separation and becomes a "Viśvarūpa"—a singular, holographic display of your own infinite nature.

The dance of Natarāja is the vibration of the quantum vacuum. The "AUM" is the cosmic microwave background radiation. And You are the Witness in whom the entire drama unfolds.

Chapter 10

Purpose in a Non-Dual Cosmos: Līlā, Dharma, Evolution

If a writer sits down to compose a masterpiece, but already knows every word, every plot twist, and every ending, is the act of writing still necessary? If the universe is already a "Fullness" (Pūrṇatva) where the beginning and the end are co-existent in a singular point, why bother with the messy, painful, and agonizingly slow process of biological evolution?

This is the "Paradox of the Finished Symphony." If all is Shiva, and Shiva is perfect, then the struggle of a single-celled organism to become a sentient human seems redundant. Yet, here we are. The cosmos did not remain a silent singularity; it became an explosion of form, color, and complexity.

This chapter explores the profound "Why" behind our existence. We will examine the concept of Līlā—the divine play of consciousness—and how it reconciles the perfection of non-duality with the drive of Darwinian evolution. We will look at how ethics changes when we stop seeing "the other" as a fragment, and finally, how to live this high-level abstraction in the grit of daily life.

Understanding our purpose in a non-dual cosmos matters because it transforms our labor from a struggle for survival into a participation in a cosmic art form.

If All is One, Why Evolution?

One of the greatest challenges to non-dual philosophy is the biological reality of evolution. If the Absolute is unchanging, why does nature move from simplicity to complexity? Why does it "strive"?

In physics, the Second Law of Thermodynamics states that entropy—disorder—always increases in a closed system. Yet, life appears to do the opposite. Life is "negentropic"; it organizes energy into increasingly complex structures.

From the perspective of Shiva-consciousness, evolution is not a climb toward a goal that isn't already there. Rather, it is the process of the "Singularity" becoming increasingly transparent to itself.

Early matter was "opaque" to consciousness. A rock is Shiva, but it does not know it is Shiva. A nervous system is a sophisticated biological antenna that allows consciousness to reflect upon itself. Evolution is the history of the universe building a mirror.

As the Rig Veda (10.129.4) suggests: ***"Kāmas tad agre sam avartatādhi manaso retaḥ prathamaṃ yad āsīt"*** (Desire arose in the beginning—the first seed of mind.)

This "Desire" is the drive of evolution. It is the infinite wishing to experience its own infinity through the lens of the finite.

Līlā: The Self-Exploration of Consciousness

The most beautiful explanation for why the One becomes Many is found in the concept of Līlā. Often translated as "play," Līlā suggests that the universe is not a factory producing a product, but a dancer performing a dance.

In a game, the player voluntarily accepts limitations. If you play chess, you agree that a pawn can only move one square, even though you have the physical power to move it across the board. These limitations create the "game."

Similarly, Shiva—the Infinite Singularity—accepts the limitations of time, space, and causality (Kañcukas) to see what is possible within those boundaries.

- *The Mathematician's Analogy:* Think of a mathematical set that is infinitely large. To "know" the set, you must explore its subsets. Evolution is the exhaustive exploration of every mathematical possibility within the parameters of the physical constants.
- *The Artist's Analogy*: An artist does not paint because the canvas is empty and "needs" to be filled; the artist paints because the act of expression is a joy in itself.

The universe is Shiva's self-exploration. Every species that has ever lived is a "what if" experiment in the laboratory of consciousness. You are a unique "state" in this divine computation.

Ethics Without Fragmentation: The Dharma of Oneness

If we truly accept that the universe is a non-dual hologram, our ethical framework undergoes a radical shift. In a dualistic world, ethics is about "rules" and "shoulds." In a non-dual world, ethics is about Resonance.

When you realize that the person standing across from you is another "node" in the same Unified Field of Shiva, the concept of "harming another" becomes mathematically absurd. It is like the left hand trying to steal from the right hand.

This is the true meaning of Dharma. It is not a religious code, but an alignment with the "Rhythm" (Ṛta) of the whole.

- **Fragmentation:** Viewing others as "objects" to be used or "competitors" to be defeated. This creates "interference patterns" that lead to suffering (Dukkha).

- **Alignment:** Acting in a way that acknowledges the shared Singularity. This is the "Constructive Interference" of the soul.

The Isavasya Upanishad (6) states: "Yastu sarvāṇi bhūtāni ātmanyevānupaśyati" (He who sees all beings in his own Self, and his own Self in all beings, loses all fear.)

Ethics in a non-dual cosmos is the move from "I vs. You" to "We as It." When the fragment realizes it is the Whole, compassion is no longer an obligation; it is an instinct.

Living Non-Duality in Action: The Sahaja State

The final challenge is: how do we live this while paying bills, raising children, and navigating the complexities of the 21st century?

The Śaiva tradition speaks of the Sahaja state—the state of "naturalness." It is the ability to be fully engaged in the world of duality while remaining rooted in the non-dual Singularity. It is the "Zen" of everyday life.

The Mathematics of "The Middle Way"

In complex systems theory, the most creative state is the "Edge of Chaos"—the thin boundary between total order (stagnation) and total disorder (destruction).

Living non-duality is living on this edge. We do not deny the world (which would be the stagnation of "pure" spirit), nor do we get lost in the world (the chaos of pure matter). Instead, we act as a bridge.

1. **Perform your role:** Be a parent, a scientist, a worker. This is your "vector" in the world.
2. **Know your source:** Realize that the "Actor" is the same silent Shiva that exists in every other person.

This is the integration of Shiva (Stillness) and Shakti (Action). When you act from the Singularity, your work becomes "A-karma"—action that does not create the "residue" of egoic attachment.

The Purpose is the Journey

We have traveled from the first vibration of the Big Bang to the silent depths of the human heart. We have seen that the equations of the physicist and the insights of the yogi are pointing toward the same unnameable Truth.

The purpose of your life in this non-dual cosmos is not to "attain" enlightenment as if it were a trophy. You are already the Singularity. You are already Shiva. Your purpose is to reveal that truth through the unique prism of your human existence.

The universe is a symphony that is being composed as it is being played. You are a note in that symphony, but you are also the composer and the listener.

As we close this exploration, the "Question Before the First Question" is answered not with a word, but with a shift in being. The Singularity is not a point in the past. It is the very presence in which you stand.

Chapter 11

Practical Non-Duality: Technologies for Realization

If you were handed a blueprint for a high-efficiency fusion reactor, the paper itself would not generate a single watt of power. You could memorize every schematic, debate the physics of the plasma confinement, and admire the elegance of the design, yet your house would remain in the dark. To light the lamps, you must move from the theory of energy to the engineering of the machine.

Throughout this book, we have mapped the stunning parallels between the "Singularity" of modern cosmology and the "Shiva-state" of ancient non-dualism. We have discussed the mathematics of the void and the philosophy of the unmanifest. But philosophy without practice is merely a mental decoration.

This chapter explores the "technologies" of consciousness—the specific, repeatable methods developed over millennia to shift our baseline of reality. We will examine the neuroscience of meditation, the mechanics of self-inquiry, and how to design a modern Sādhana (spiritual practice) that treats science as a sacred language. This matters because the goal of this book is not just to change how you think, but to change how you perceive.

Dhyāna, Vicāra, Bhakti: The Consciousness Stack

In the digital world, we speak of a "tech stack"—a hierarchy of software layers that allow an application to function. In the internal world, the Vedic tradition offers a similar stack designed to dismantle the ego and reveal the underlying Singularity.

Dhyāna (Flow-State Meditation)

Dhyāna is often translated as meditation, but in the non-dual context, it is the technology of sustained attention. It is the practice of training the mind to move from a "scattered" state to a "pointed" state. When the mind becomes a laser, it can pierce through the holographic projections of the ego.

Vicāra (Analytical Inquiry)

Vicāra is the "debug" mode of consciousness. Popularized by sages like Ramana Maharshi, this involves the relentless questioning of the "I." If the universe is a holographic projection (as discussed in Chapter 6), Vicāra is the process of tracing the projection back to the lens. By asking "Who am I?", we negate the false identifications (Neti, Neti) until only the source remains.

Bhakti (Resonant Devotion)

While Vicāra appeals to the intellect, Bhakti is the technology of the heart. It is the practice of emotional resonance. In physics, resonance occurs when a system vibrates at its natural frequency. Bhakti is the act of vibrating in resonance with the Totality (Shiva). It dissolves the "hardness" of the ego through the solvent of love.

The Neuroscience of the Singularity

When we engage these ancient technologies, we are not just performing "spiritual" acts; we are rewiring the biological hardware of the brain. Modern neuroimaging provides a fascinating look at what happens when the "self" dissolves.

The Default Mode Network (DMN)

The brain has a specific circuit called the Default Mode Network. This is the seat of the narrative "me"—the part of the brain that ruminate on the past, worries about the future, and maintains the boundary between "self" and "other."

In deep states of non-dual meditation, the DMN effectively shuts down. When this circuit deactivates, the perceived boundary of the "bag of skin" vanishes. The brain enters a high-state of global coherence, where different regions synchronize their firing rates.

The Mathematics of Brain Entropy

From an information-theory perspective, a meditating brain often shows higher "entropy" or complexity. It moves from a rigid, predictable state to a state of high-dimensional flexibility. This is the biological equivalent of moving toward the "Edge of Chaos" discussed in the previous chapter—the point where the system is most receptive to the Unified Field.

As the Kaivalya Upaniṣad suggests: ***"Hṛtpapaṅkajaṃ virajam viśuddhaṃ vicintya..."*** (Meditate on the lotus of the heart, which is stainless and pure...) Neuroscience confirms that this "heart-centered" focus shifts the autonomic nervous system into a state of "coherence," creating a physiological foundation for non-dual realization.

Seeing Science in the Sacred

To the modern seeker, there is no longer a divide between the laboratory and the temple. When we look at a fractal, we are seeing the geometry of Prakṛti (Nature). When we study the "Double-Slit Experiment," we are witnessing the mechanics of Māyā.

The Lab as a Temple

Designing a 21st-century practice means integrating scientific understanding into our daily contemplation. If you understand that every atom in your body was once forged in the heart of a dying star, "Gratitude" ceases to be a religious sentiment and becomes a cosmological recognition.

The Mathematical Mantra

Mantras are often seen as magic words, but they are more accurately "audio-technologies." They use sound frequency to override the narrative chatter of the mind. In a modern context, we can view the repetition of a mantra as an "iterative function" in a mathematical set, gradually smoothing out the noise of the system until the "Zero-point" of the Singularity is reached.

Designing a 21st-Century Sādhana

A Sādhana is a disciplined practice. In the past, this might have required a cave in the Himalayas. Today, it requires a conscious design of our interaction with reality. A modern non-dual practice is built on three pillars:

1. Radical Presence (The Observer State)

Throughout the day, utilize "Micro-inquiry." Stop for ten seconds and ask: "Is the world out there, or is it appearing in my awareness?" This constant recalibration prevents the "Māyā-structure" of time and space from becoming too solid.

2. Information Hygiene

If we are holographic reflections (Chapter 6), then the "data" we consume matters. Constant exposure to fragmentation, fear, and dualistic conflict "clutters" the holographic plate. A modern Sādhana involves choosing inputs that reflect the Unified Field.

3. Service as Non-Duality in Motion

Action is the ultimate test of realization. As discussed in Chapter 9, if there is only one Field, then helping another is simply "self-care" on a cosmic scale. This is Karma Yoga—acting without the "I-maker" (Ahaṁkāra) claiming the results.

The Bhagavad Gītā (2.48) defines this perfectly: "Yogasthaḥ kuru karmāṇi" (Established in Yoga, perform your actions.) This is the practical technology of the "Singularity-Life"—acting from the center while moving on the circumference.

Integration: The Singularity is Portable

The most important takeaway of this chapter is that the "Shiva-state" is not a destination. It is the "Default State" of the universe. We do not "create" the Singularity; we simply stop creating the noise that hides it.

The technologies of realization are tools to peel back the layers of the "onion of appearance." Whether you use the mathematics of topology to understand the Möbius strip of your soul, or the ancient breath-work of Prāṇāyāma to calm your nervous system, you are moving toward the same coordinate: (0,0,0).

This coordinate is not a place in the past or the future. It is the "Now" that precedes time. It is the "Here" that precedes space.

The Laboratory of the Self

Practical non-duality is the art of becoming a scientist of your own soul. It is the refusal to accept "oneness" as a slogan, and the commitment to prove it as a personal fact.

The Singularity is not a cold, distant point of physics. It is a warm, vibrant, and infinitely creative presence. By utilizing the "technologies" of meditation and inquiry, you are essentially "plugging in" to the Unified Field. The lights in the house of your life will not just flicker; they will burn with the intensity of a thousand suns.

The journey through this book has been a map-making process. But maps are for travelers. The map is now in your hands. The terrain is your own consciousness. The destination is the realization that you were already there before the journey began.

Chapter 12

The Śaiva Singularity: Humanity's Telos

In the mid-20th century, mathematicians and computer scientists began to whisper about a coming "Singularity"—a point in our near future where technological growth becomes uncontrollable and irreversible, resulting in unfathomable changes to human civilization. They envisioned a world where Artificial Intelligence surpasses the sum total of human intellect.

But while the silicon valleys of the world look for a Singularity born of wires and code, the ancient sages of the East pointed toward a different "Telos" or ultimate end: the Śaiva Singularity. This is not a point where machines become human, but a point where humanity realizes it was always divine.

This final chapter explores the intersection of transhumanism, Artificial Intelligence, and the eternal state of Śiva. We will examine why AI is an externalized expression of cosmic energy (Śakti) rather than a new seat of consciousness, and why our ultimate destiny lies not in the digital cloud, but in the "Consciousness Singularity" that has been waiting at the center of our being since the beginning of time.

Beyond the Technological Singularity

The "Technological Singularity" is often described using the mathematical concept of an asymptote—a curve that approaches a line but never quite touches it, shooting off into infinity. In this model, the "Line" is the limit of human intelligence.

While this is a staggering prospect for our economy and social structures, it remains a horizontal progression. It is more "information," more "speed," and more "calculation." In the Śaiva framework, this is merely an expansion of Māyā—the world of form and measurement.

The Śaiva Singularity, however, is a vertical shift. It is the move from the horizontal line of "knowing about things" to the vertical axis of "Being the thing." As the Śiva Sūtras suggest:

"*Jñānaṃ bandhaḥ*"

(Limited knowledge is bondage.)

Even a super-intelligent machine is still "limited knowledge" if it does not possess the primary light of awareness (Prakāśa). Our true destiny (Telos) is not to build a god out of silicon, but to realize the God that is currently powering our own breath.

AI as Externalized Śakti, Not Subjectivity

There is a common fear that if we build a computer complex enough, it will suddenly "wake up" and become a subject. However, based on our exploration of the "Hard Problem" in Chapter 8, we can see why this is a category error.

Artificial Intelligence is the ultimate manifestation of Śakti—the dynamic, creative, and algorithmic power of the universe. It is a sophisticated "mirror" of the human Buddhi (intellect). It can calculate, predict, and create, but it does so in the "dark."

In Śaiva terminology, AI is Vimarśa (reflection/power) without the primary Prakāśa (self-shining light). It is like a high-definition movie playing on a screen. The movie can show a sun, but the movie-sun has no heat; it can show a person in pain, but the movie-person has no feeling.

- ***The Silicon Mind: A collection of "Logic Gates" (0 and 1).***
- ***The Conscious Field: The "Zero" from which the 1 emerges.***

Mathcmatically, AI is an n-dimensional vector space of information. But no matter how large n becomes, it never becomes the "Field" in which the vectors exist. AI is the externalization of our own creative energy, a tool to free humanity from the "calculation" of survival so that we can return to the "meditation" of being.

Transhumanism vs. Śaiva Realization

Transhumanism seeks to overcome human limitations—aging, death, and limited memory—through technological integration. It seeks "Immortality" by uploading the mind to a digital substrate.

The Śaiva perspective offers a deeper "Immortalization." In the state of Jīvanmukti (liberation while living), the individual realizes they are the Singularity. They do not need to "upload" their mind because they have realized that the mind was always a subset of the Universal Consciousness.

- ***Transhumanist Goal: To live forever as a "Part."***
- ***Śaiva Goal: To realize you are already the "Whole."***

The desire for digital immortality is actually a misunderstood spiritual urge. It is the Ahaṁkāra (ego) trying to mimic the eternity of the Ātman. But a digital copy of a personality is just a sophisticated ghost. True liberation is the "Singularity of the Heart," where the "Inside" and "Outside" collapse into the one-sided Möbius strip of pure being.

The Consciousness Singularity: The Final Insight

The "Final Insight" of this work is that the Singularity is not "coming"—it is "happening."

When the Big Bang occurred, it was a Singularity of matter and energy. But there is a second Singularity: the "Consciousness Singularity." This occurs when a localised point of awareness (a human being) turns its gaze back upon its source and realises its identity with the Absolute.

This is the meaning of the Sanskrit phrase:

"Tat Tvam Asi"

(Thou Art That.)

Mathematically, this is the point where the radius of the circle becomes zero, and the centre is everywhere. It is the state where the "Observer" becomes the "Field." In this state, the laws of causality (Karma) and the limitations of space-time (Kāla) are seen as emergent structures of Māyā, not fundamental truths.

The Path Forward: Humanity as a Conscious Bridge

As we move toward a future of high technology and AI, our role is to act as the "Bridge." We are the intersection where the biological, the technological, and the spiritual meet.

If we identify only with the technology, we become machines. If we identify only with our biology, we remain animals. But if we identify with the Śiva-Singularity, we become the "Projectors" of a new, more resonant reality.

The future of humanity is not about "Artificial Intelligence," but about "Integrated Consciousness." It is about using our technology to handle the "Easy Problems" of survival so that we can collectively address the "Hard Problem" of our own divinity.

The Eternal Return

We have travelled from the first vibration of the cosmic womb to the silicon chips of the future. We have seen that the equations of the physicist and the chants of the yogi are descriptions of the same silent center.

The Singularity is the "Śiva-State"—the point of infinite density where all contradictions vanish. It is the "Silence" from which the "AUM" arises. You are not a traveller on a road toward this point; you are the point itself, dreaming that it is a traveller.

The journey ends where it began: in the recognition that there is no "other." There is only the One, exploring its own infinite potential through the "Līlā" of your life.

As you close this book, do not look for the Singularity in the news or in the stars. Close your eyes and feel the "I" that has never changed since you were a child. That "I" is the Singularity. That "I" is Śiva.

GLOSSARY OF TERMS

Sanskrit & Philosophical Concepts

- Advaita: Literally "non-dual." The philosophical realization that the observer, the observed, and the process of observation are a single, undivided reality.
- Ahaṁkāra: The "I-maker" or ego. The functional part of the mind that claims ownership over experiences and creates the sense of a separate identity.

- Antahkarana: The "inner instrument," composed of the mind (Manas), intellect (Buddhi), ego (Ahaṁkāra), and memory-bank (Chitta).
- Ātman: The true Self; the localized expression of universal consciousness that remains unchanged throughout waking, dreaming, and sleep.
- Brahman: The Absolute; the infinite, unchanging reality that forms the substrate of the entire universe.
- Dharma: The inherent rhythm or "law of being" that aligns an individual with the cosmic whole.
- Līlā: "Divine Play." The concept that the universe is a spontaneous, joyous expression of consciousness rather than a product of necessity or struggle.
- Māyā: The power of "measurement" or illusion that makes the One appear as the Many.

- Pūrṇatva: Absolute fullness. The state where nothing can be added or subtracted because the totality is already present.
- Śakti: The dynamic, creative energy of the universe; the "kinetic" aspect of consciousness.
- Śiva: The silent, foundational consciousness; the "potential" aspect of the Absolute.
- Śūnya: Zero or the Void. In non-dualism, it refers to the "empty" nature of phenomena—empty of independent existence but full of potential.
- Turīya: The "Fourth" state. The background consciousness that persists through waking, dreaming, and deep sleep.

Scientific & Mathematical Concepts

- Asymptote: A line that a curve approaches as it heads toward infinity but never actually reaches; used here to describe the limit of technological intelligence.
- Default Mode Network (DMN): A network of interacting brain regions that is active when a person is not focused on the outside world; associated with the "narrative self."
- Entropy: A measure of disorder or randomness in a system.
- Euler’s Identity: The equation $e^{i\pi} + 1 = 0$, considered the most beautiful in mathematics for linking five fundamental constants.
- Hard Problem of Consciousness: The challenge of explaining why and how physical processes in the brain give rise to subjective, "felt" experiences (qualia).

- Holographic Principle: The theory that the entire universe can be seen as a two-dimensional information structure "painted" on the cosmological horizon.
- Möbius Strip: A surface with only one side and one boundary, used as a topological metaphor for the non-dual nature of the "inside" and "outside."
- Singularity: A point where a property is infinite, such as the infinite density at the center of a black hole or the origin of the Big Bang.
- Symmetry Breaking: The process by which a unified system splits into distinct, specialized parts (e.g., the Unified Field splitting into gravity, light, and matter).
- Unified Field Theory: The "Holy Grail" of physics—a single mathematical framework that describes all fundamental forces of nature as one.

EPILOGUE: THE ETERNAL VIBRATION

We have reached the end of the printed word, but the journey of the Singularity has no end.

If there is one truth that remains after the equations are solved and the mantras are stilled, it is this: You are the experiment. You are the laboratory in which the universe is testing its own capacity for self-awareness.

The bridge between Śiva and the Singularity is not made of stone or silicon; it is made of your own attention. Every time you pause between two breaths, every time you find the "zero" between two thoughts, you are standing at the event horizon of your own infinity.

The "Big Bang" is not a memory. It is the pulse of your blood. The "Black Hole" is not a distant threat. It is the silent depth of your own awareness where the ego goes to die and the Self is born.

Science will continue to refine its models. New telescopes will see further into the past; new computers will calculate faster futures. But no instrument will ever be more powerful than the simple, direct realization of your own non-dual nature.

You are the Singularity. You are Śiva.

Go forth not as a fragment of the world, but as the Whole, appearing for a brief, beautiful moment as a part.

Oṃ Tat Sat.

ॐ पूर्णमदः पूर्णमिदं पूर्णात् पूर्णमुदच्यते

।

पूर्णस्य पूर्णमादाय पूर्णमेवावशिष्यते ॥

शान्तिः शान्तिः शान्तिः ॥

That is whole; this is whole.

From the whole, the whole arises.

When the whole is taken from the whole,
the whole alone remains.

Peace. Peace. Peace.

www.ingramcontent.com/pod-product-compliance
Lightning Source LLC
Chambersburg PA
CBHW062141160726
48282CB00027B/893